Nature's Wonders

THE NILE

ANN HEINRICHS

WITHDRAWN

 **Marshall Cavendish**
Benchmark
New York

Marshall Cavendish Benchmark
99 White Plains Road
Tarrytown, NY 10591-5502
www.marshallcavendish.us

Expert Reader: Dr. Alan Nicol, research fellow and head of Water Policy Programme, Overseas Development Institute, London; consultant on Nile Basin development matters for several international agencies

Library of Congress Cataloging-in-Publication Data
Heinrichs, Ann.
The Nile / by Ann Heinrichs. — 1st ed.
p. cm. — (Nature's wonders)
Summary: "Provides comprehensive information on the geography, history, wildlife, peoples, and environmental issues of the Nile River basin"—Provided by publisher
Includes bibliographical references and index.
ISBN 978-0-7614-2854-1
1. Nile River Valley—Juvenile literature. I. Title.
DT115.H45 2008
962—dc22
2007019187

Editor: Christine Florie
Publisher: Michelle Bisson
Art Director: Anahid Hamparian
Series Designer: Kay Petronio

Photo research by Connie Gardner

Cover photo by Gerry Ellis/Minden Pictures

The photographs in this book are used by permission and through the courtesy of: *Art Resource:* Erich Lessing, 4, 10, 23, 43; Scala, 41; Snark, 47; *AP Photo:* Alfred de Montesquiou, 84-85; *Getty Images:* David S. Boyer, 5; Robert Caputo, 11; Galio Images/Aquavision, 14-15; AFP, 16; Randy Olson, 18; Sylvain Grandadam, 25; Nasa/Digital, 29; Beverly Joubert, 80-81; Panoramic Images, 87; *Danita Delimont:* John Warburton, 28, 50; American Art and Architecture, 56; *Art Archive:* British Museum/Dagli Orti, 29; *Minden Pictures:* Frans Lanting, 33, 36 (B), back cover; Michael and Patricia Fogden, 35; Jim Brandenburg, 37; *The Granger Collection:* 40, 44; *The Image Works:* Mary Evans Picture Library, 59; *Photo Researchers Inc.:* Georg Gerster, 66; *Corbis:* David Bartruff, 7; Nevada Wier, 12, 39; Yann Arthus-Bertrand, 24; Werner Forman, 31; Robert and Lori Franz, 32; Roger Tidman, 34 (T); Paul A. Souders, 34 (B), Martin Harvey, 36 (T); Arthur Aslimue, 52; Ed Kashi, 54; Caroline Penn, 60; Stapleton Collection, 23, 62; Lloyd Cluff, 65; Reza Webistan, 69; Lawson Wood, 70; Jonathan Blair, 70; Bojan Breceli, 76; Michael S. Lewis, 88; Fridmar Damm/zefa, 89 (T); *Super Stock Photos:* age/footstock, 8, 89 (B); SuperStock, 20; *Alamy:* Robert Harding Picture Library Ltd., 19; the Print Collection, 46; *Photo Researchers:* Tom McHugh, 78; *Art Archive:* British Museum/Dagli Orti, 29; *Minden Pictures:* Frans Lanting, 33; 36 (B), back cover; Michael and Patricia Fogden, 35; Jim Brandenburg, 37; *The Granger Collection:* 40, 44; *The Image Works:* Mary Evans Picture Library, 59; *Photo Researchers:* Tom McHugh, 78.

Maps by Mapping Specialits Limited

Printed in China
1 3 5 6 4 2

CONTENTS

ONE

The Gift of the Nile

The Nile River is the longest river in the world. Rising in the high-lands of Africa's interior, it flows north through Sudan and Egypt to its mouth at the Mediterranean Sea. Estimates of the Nile's length vary. Still, it is at least 4,160 miles (6,695 kilometers) long. That is more than one-and-a-half times the width of the continental United States.

One of the world's greatest civilizations grew up along the Nile. More than five thousand years ago ancient Egyptians developed a complex culture. Religion, arts, literature, science, and technology flourished there. Under the rule of powerful pharaohs, the Egyptians built monuments that still astonish people today.

Pharaoh Ramses II had two temples carved from the solid rock along the Nile's west bank in the 1200s B.C.E.

 The Nile River is a constant source of water, enabling civilizations to grow along its shores.

Supporting this culture was a thriving agricultural system. It relied solely on the waters of the Nile. Every year the river flooded its banks, leaving rich, black mud behind. The Nile itself was seen as a bountiful god, nourishing the land with its waters.

Up and Down the Nile

We think of "up" as north and "down" as south. But if you sail *up* the Nile, you are sailing south. If you sail *down* the Nile, you are sailing north. These terms were used in ancient times as well. The kingdom of Upper Egypt was in the southern part of the country, while Lower Egypt was in the north.

The Nile River flows from south to north. Does this mean it flows uphill? No—the river simply follows the law of gravity. Its waters originate at high elevations. As the land gradually slopes down to the Mediterranean Sea, the water flows downhill—which is north. The Nile is the only major river in the world that flows from south to north.

On the west bank of the Nile at Luxor, Egypt, crops thrive along the river's fertile floodplain.

A FERTILE STRIP

Without the Nile River, northern Africa would be one vast desert. That desert would stretch from the Red Sea on the east to the Atlantic Ocean on the west. In most of Egypt and northern Sudan it is not unusual for a year to pass with no rainfall. The Nile provides a fertile strip of farmland in this arid region.

The ancient Greek historian Herodotus called Egypt "the gift of the Nile." He meant that the Nile gave Egypt its very life. Without the river, there would be no Egypt at all.

Even today, about 95 percent of Egypt's population lives within

Longest and Largest

The Amazon River of South America is the world's second-longest river, after the Nile. However, the Amazon is considered the world's largest river in terms of the volume of water it carries.

Cairo, Egypt, is located on the banks of the Nile River, just south of the Nile Delta.

a few miles of the Nile. Cairo, Egypt's capital, grew up along the Nile. It has become the largest city in Africa. Still, Egypt is not the only country that relies on the Nile.

WATER FOR MILLIONS

Two great rivers—the White Nile and the Blue Nile—come together to form the main Nile River. These two **tributaries** meet at Khartoum, the capital of Sudan. By the time they meet, the White and Blue Niles have

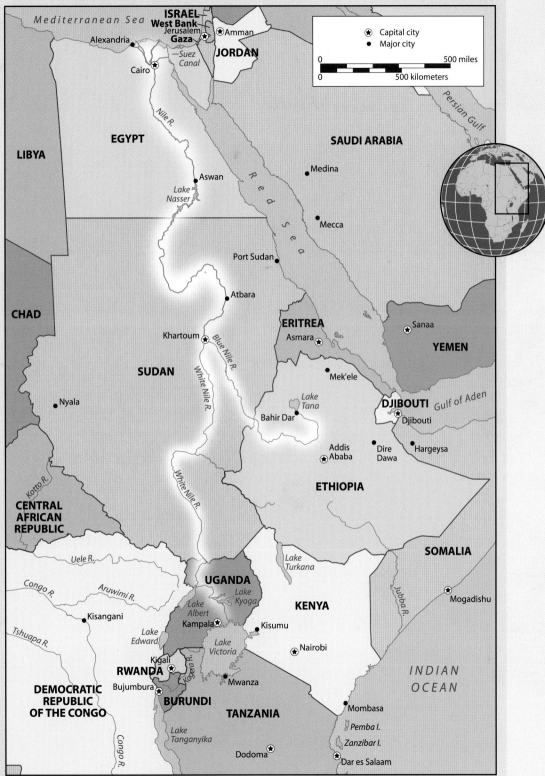

Mediterranean Sea

ISRAEL
West Bank
Jerusalem
Gaza
Amman
JORDAN

Alexandria

Suez Canal

Cairo

LIBYA

EGYPT

Nile R.

Aswan

Lake Nasser

SAUDI ARABIA

Medina

Mecca

Red Sea

Port Sudan

CHAD

Atbara

ERITREA

Asmara

YEMEN

Sanaa

Khartoum

Blue Nile R.

SUDAN

White Nile R.

Mek'ele

Lake Tana

DJIBOUTI

Djibouti

Gulf of Aden

Nyala

Bahir Dar

Addis Ababa

Dire Dawa

Hargeysa

ETHIOPIA

Kotto R.

CENTRAL
AFRICAN
REPUBLIC

White Nile R.

SOMALIA

Uele R.

Lake Turkana

Congo R.

Aruwimi R.

UGANDA

Lake Kyoga

Mogadishu

Kisangani

Lake Albert

Kampala

KENYA

Kisumu

Jubba R.

Tshuapa R.

Lake Edward

Kigali

Lake Victoria

Nairobi

RWANDA

Kagera R.

INDIAN
OCEAN

DEMOCRATIC
REPUBLIC
OF THE CONGO

Bujumbura

BURUNDI

Mwanza

TANZANIA

Mombasa

Congo R.

Lake Tanganyika

Pemba I.

Zanzibar I.

Dodoma

Dar es Salaam

Persian Gulf

★ Capital city
● Major city

0 — 500 miles
0 — 500 kilometers

For the people who live along the Nile, their life is a combination of old ways and new challenges.

gathered waters from ten countries. Altogether, the Nile River's **drainage basin** covers about one-tenth of Africa's land area. It is estimated that more than 160 million people depend on the waters that contribute to the Nile for survival.

In some ways life along the Nile is the same as it has always been. Peasant farmers raise their crops, and herders bring their cattle to drink. In other ways life has radically changed. Ancient Egypt was a rich and powerful land. The kingdom of Nubia, south of Egypt, was wealthy as well. Today, however, the Nile basin countries are among the poorest in the world. Their populations are growing fast, and so is their need for water.

With greater demands on the Nile, its **ecosystems** face serious threats. Wetlands, wildlife, and water quality can easily become low priorities. Both the Nile basin countries and the world community are aware of these dangers. Together, they hope to preserve this river, which has enriched human life for thousands of years.

The Nile River begins at the meeting place of the White Nile and Blue Nile rivers. ▶▶

TWO

Two Sources, Winding Courses

For centuries people believed the Nile River had just one source. They thought its waters must rise somewhere in central Africa. Only in the late 1800s did it become clear that two long rivers join to form the Nile.

The White Nile is not exactly white. Neither is the Blue Nile blue. Then how did these rivers get their names? The White Nile takes on a grayish-white color from the clay it picks up along its course. In contrast, the waters of the Blue Nile are pure and clear for most of the year.

These two rivers follow vastly different patterns. The White Nile is the longest of the Nile's tributaries. It carries waters that originate in eight countries. However, the White Nile contributes only about 14 percent of the Nile River's waters. The remaining 86 percent comes from the Blue Nile and other Ethiopian rivers.

◀ *The Blue Nile River flows from Ethiopia's Lake Tana into Sudan, where it merges with the White Nile to form the Nile River.*

THE WHITE NILE

The continent of North America has its Great Lakes. They lie on the border between the United States and Canada. The continent of Africa has its great lakes, too. They lie south of the equator, in the highlands of east-central Africa. Here, in this great lakes region, rises the White Nile.

Among the African great lakes, the largest is Lake Victoria. It borders the countries of Uganda, Tanzania, and Kenya. In terms of the area it covers, this vast body of water is the largest lake in Africa. It is also one of the largest freshwater lakes in the world. Lake Victoria—discovered by Europeans only in 1858—is the primary source of the White Nile.

Finding a river's source can be a complicated matter. The source might be an underground spring, a collection of streams, or the melting ice of a glacier. Quite often a river's source is a lake, such as Lake Victoria. However, that lake itself may receive its waters from other rivers that flow into it. These rivers are called feeder rivers or headstreams. Taking the longest headstream and tracing it back to its beginning, you find the lake's headwaters—the most distant point at which its waters originate. The headwaters are the ultimate source of a river or lake.

In the case of Lake Victoria, only the White Nile flows out of it. But many rivers and streams feed their waters into the lake. The largest of those feeder rivers is the Kagera River. But where do the Kagera's waters originate? The answer to that question resolves three issues:

1. Where are the headwaters of Lake Victoria?

2. Where are the headwaters of the White Nile? and finally (since the White Nile is the Nile River's longest tributary),

3. Where are the headwaters of the great Nile River itself?

Lake Victoria, at 26,800 square miles (69,480 sq km), is the main body of water that is drained by the Nile River.

On March 31, 2006, researchers marked the location of the source of the Nile in the Nyungwe rain forest in Rwanda.

FROM A TRICKLE TO KHARTOUM

Deep in the Nyungwe rain forest of Rwanda, water trickles from a muddy hole. Rains from the forest add to this trickle, forming the Rukarara River. These waters are believed to be the most remote headwaters of the White Nile.

Eventually, water from the Rukarara enters the Kagera River. The Kagera, in turn, empties into Lake Victoria near Bukoba, Tanzania. For many years the Luvironza River in Burundi was believed to be the White Nile's remotest headstream. Only in 2006 did explorers discover a more distant headstream—the Rukarara— and its trickling headwaters.

Many other feeder rivers contribute their waters to Lake Victoria and to other lakes farther downstream. As a result the White Nile contains water that has passed through Rwanda, Burundi, Tanzania, Uganda, Kenya, and the Congo.

This watercourse may seem like a long journey, but for the White Nile, it is only the beginning. The White Nile leaves Lake Victoria near Jinja, Uganda. (The river once tumbled over the dramatic Ripon Falls. However, when the Owen Falls Dam was built in 1954, the waterfall became submerged.) The river follows a generally north-ward course, flowing through Uganda's Lake Kyoga and Lake Albert.

River of Many Names

When the White Nile leaves Lake Victoria, it is known as the Victoria Nile. When it exits Lake Albert, it is called the Albert Nile. Once the White Nile enters Sudan, it is known as Bahr al-Jabal, Arabic for "River of the Mountains." On leaving Lake No, the river is called Bahr al-Abyad, or "White Nile."

The Sudd's heavy vegetation creates many channels that cannot be navigated and hinders the flow of water to Sudan and Egypt.

Continuing northward, the White Nile leaves Uganda and enters Sudan. There it travels through a vast swampland called the Sudd (Arabic for "barrier"). At the north end of the Sudd the White Nile passes through a lagoon called Lake No, where it is joined by the Bahr al-Ghazal. Farther downstream, the Sobat River enters from its origins in the Ethiopian highlands. Then the White Nile proceeds to Khartoum, the capital of Sudan. There, at last, it joins the Blue Nile to form the waterway we know as the Nile River.

THE BLUE NILE

The source and course of the Blue Nile are much more straightforward. Lake Tana, in the highlands of northwestern Ethiopia, is the source of the Blue Nile. Ethiopians call the Blue Nile Abay or Abbay, meaning "river."

Dozens of streams flow into Lake Tana. Of those the longest is a stream called the Little Abay or Little Blue Nile. About 85 miles (137 km) above the lake, the Little Abay begins as a bubbling spring called the Springs of Sakala. This spring is considered to be the headwaters of the Blue Nile.

The Blue Nile flows for about 1,000 miles (1,609 km) before it meets with the White Nile at Khartoum, to form the main Nile River.

In a high, mountain-side meadow above Lake Tana, near the village of Gishe Abay, a sparkling spring of water bubbles from the ground. This is the Springs of Sakala. Ethiopians call the spring the sacred source of the Blue Nile. It is considered a holy place, and villagers fill their bottles with its water to use in blessings and remedies.

Near the town of Bahir Dar, the Blue Nile leaves Lake Tana, heading south. Soon it cascades over the spectacular Blue Nile Falls. The waters, crashing over a steep cliff, send up a misty spray that often filters sunlight as a rainbow. Ethiopians call this waterfall Tissisat, meaning "Smoke of Fire." (The flow of the falls has been greatly reduced since 2003 due to a hydroelectricity project.)

Next, the Blue Nile rushes through a series of rapids before plunging into the Blue Nile Gorge. This deep canyon curves south and west through Ethiopia before entering Sudan. Once in Sudan the Blue Nile flows northwest until it meets the White Nile at Khartoum.

The Blue Nile Falls drop more than 150 feet (45 m) into the gorge below.

Flow Patterns

The Nile River's longest tributary is the White Nile. So why does the Blue Nile contribute more water to the Nile? The answer lies in the very different flow patterns of the two tributaries.

The White Nile is fed by year-round rains. These waters are stored in lakes, especially Lake Victoria. The White Nile's waters flow fairly steadily out of the lakes. But once the river reaches the vast Sudd swamp, its waters meander through the wetland for more than a year. During that time more than half of the White Nile's water is lost through evaporation.

The Blue Nile, on the other hand, has a far more seasonal flow. During dry seasons or droughts the Blue Nile has a very weak flow. However, from July through September, heavy **monsoon** rains drench the Ethiopian highlands. These seasonal rains send a flood of waters rushing downstream, containing close to 60 percent of the main Nile's annual flow. The floodwaters reach the main Nile River with little loss in volume.

PHYSICAL MAP OF THE NILE RIVER BASIN

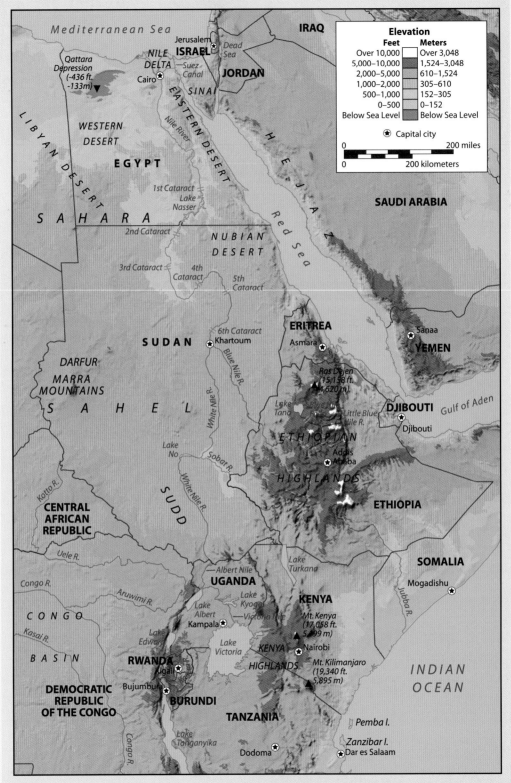

Mediterranean Sea

Qattara Depression (-436 ft. -133m)▼

Jerusalem
ISRAEL
Dead Sea
IRAQ

NILE DELTA
Suez Canal
Cairo ★
JORDAN

SINAI

Nile River

WESTERN DESERT

LIBYAN DESERT

EGYPT

EASTERN DESERT

SAHARA

1st Cataract
Lake Nasser

2nd Cataract

3rd Cataract
4th Cataract
5th Cataract

NUBIAN DESERT

H E J A Z

Red Sea

SAUDI ARABIA

6th Cataract
Khartoum ★

SUDAN

Blue Nile R.

ERITREA
Asmara ★

Sanaa ★
YEMEN

DARFUR
MARRA MOUNTAINS

S A H E L

White Nile R.

Ras Dejen (15,158 ft. 4,620 m) ▲

Lake Tana

Little Blue Nile R.
Blue Nile R.

DJIBOUTI
Djibouti ★

Gulf of Aden

ETHIOPIAN

Addis Ababa ★

HIGHLANDS

ETHIOPIA

Lake No

Sobat R.

White Nile R.

S U D D

CENTRAL AFRICAN REPUBLIC

Kotto R.

Uele R.

Lake Turkana

SOMALIA

Mogadishu ★

Albert Nile
UGANDA

Congo R.

Aruwimi R.

C O N G O

Kasai R.

B A S I N

Lake Albert
Lake Kyoga
Victoria Nile
Kampala ★

Lake Edward

Lake Victoria

RWANDA
Kigali ★

Bujumbura ★

BURUNDI

DEMOCRATIC REPUBLIC OF THE CONGO

Congo R.

Lake Tanganyika

Dodoma ★

TANZANIA

KENYA

Mt. Kenya (17,058 ft. 5,199 m) ▲

KENYA HIGHLANDS

Nairobi ★

Mt. Kilimanjaro (19,340 ft. 5,895 m) ▲

Jubba R.

INDIAN OCEAN

Pemba I.

Zanzibar I.
Dar es Salaam ★

Elevation

Feet	Meters
Over 10,000	Over 3,048
5,000–10,000	1,524–3,048
2,000–5,000	610–1,524
1,000–2,000	305–610
500–1,000	152–305
0–500	0–152
Below Sea Level	Below Sea Level

★ Capital city

0 ___ 200 miles
0 ___ 200 kilometers

KHARTOUM: AT LAST, THE BEGINNING

Only here, at Khartoum, does the Nile River itself truly begin. From Khartoum, the Nile flows north through Sudan into Egypt. Along the way the river undergoes several "events."

North of Khartoum the Nile makes an S-shaped curve through the Nubian Desert. The river bends back toward the southwest before turning north again. This is called the Great Bend of the Nile. At the bend the Nile is joined by one more tributary—the Atbara River. Like the Blue Nile, the Atbara rises in the highlands of Ethiopia. It receives waters from both Ethiopia and Eritrea.

The Nile also rushes over six so-called cataracts. The usual meaning of cataract is "waterfall," but the cataracts of the Nile are more like rapids. They are shallow stretches of water broken by large stones and rocky islands. Five of the cataracts are in Sudan, while one is in Egypt. With water swirling dangerously around the rocks, the cataracts have always been major obstacles for boats on the Nile.

The Nile River flows through six natural rapids, or cataracts. This is the first cataract found between Aswan and Khartoum.

Because of the construction of the Aswan High Dam, 136,977,000 acre-feet of the Nile's waters are held back in Lake Nasser. When fed downstream, 800,000 acres of land can be irrigated.

Just south of the Sudan-Egypt border the Nile opens out into Lake Nasser (Sudan's portion of the lake is often called Lake Nubia). This lake is one of the largest artificial lakes in the world. It stores water held back by the Aswan High Dam, which was built across the Nile in 1970, just south of the Egyptian city of Aswan.

Beyond Aswan the Nile continues its northward course through the desert. Thanks to irrigation water from the Nile, farmers in the Nile Valley can raise a variety of crops. In northern Egypt the Nile passes through Cairo, the capital of modern-day Egypt. At this point the river is nearing its mouth, at the Mediterranean Sea.

Ancient Kingdoms

In ancient times several great kingdoms flourished along the Nile between Khartoum and the Mediterranean Sea. The kingdom of Nubia lay along the Nile between Khartoum and Aswan. The kingdom of Upper Egypt stretched north from Aswan almost all the way to Cairo. Aswan, Luxor, and Thebes were important cultural centers in Upper Egypt.

To the north was the kingdom of Lower Egypt. Many famous monuments were built there in ancient times. Just outside of Cairo, on the Giza Plateau, are the Sphinx (above), the Great Pyramid, and other large monuments.

Through the Delta to the Sea

North of Cairo the Nile spreads out into the broad, fertile Nile Delta. To ancient Egyptians the fan-shaped delta was the shape of a lotus flower, a symbol of new life. Actually, the delta is named after the fourth letter of the Greek alphabet—Δ (delta)—because of its triangular shape.

In ancient times the Nile split into seven branches in the delta. Today, the Nile flows across the delta in two main branches. The Rosetta branch forks to the west, while the Damietta branch angles toward the east. Between these branches the low-lying delta contains rich, black **silt** deposited by the Nile. Wetlands are scattered throughout the delta, too, and water gathers in several lakes there.

At last the mighty Nile River empties into the Mediterranean Sea. From its highest headwaters it has traveled more than 4,170 miles (6,710 km). And it has gathered waters from ten countries along the way.

A photo from space shows the massive scope and shape of the Nile Delta.

THREE

Animals and Plants of the Nile

Ancient Egyptians richly illustrated the walls of their tombs and other monuments. Their artwork shows activities such as farming, fishing, and wild game hunting. That is how we know about the great variety of animals that once lived in and around the Nile.

Wild animals such as lions, cheetahs, and antelope inhabited the deserts and grasslands beyond the Nile. In the cool mornings and evenings they came down to the river to drink. Hunters shot them with bows and arrows or captured them with nets. Hippopotamuses wallowed on the riverbanks, and

This wall painting from an ancient Egyptian tomb illustrates birds found along the Nile ca. 1400 B.C.E.

◄ *Many animals and plants thrive along the banks of the Nile River.*

crocodiles lurked in the waters. Turtles and frogs lived by the riverside, too. Bird life along the Nile included herons, ibises, cranes, ducks, and geese. Vultures and falcons soared overhead. While some birds were protected because they were considered sacred, hunters could shoot ducks and geese. Egyptians also domesticated, or tamed, ducks and geese and kept them as farm animals. The colorful Nile goose roamed freely through people's gardens and homes.

People fished in the Nile for carp, perch, and catfish. Mullet, tilapia, sturgeon, and eel were some other Nile catches. Only the common people ate fish, though. The pharaohs and other nobles were forbidden to consume fish for religious reasons. In some locations certain fish could not be eaten because they were considered sacred.

SACRED ANIMALS

For the ancient Egyptians certain animals had symbolic meanings. Various animals were associated with good fortune, rich harvests, power, danger, protection, and so on. Figures of these animals were used to represent gods.

The ibis, for example, arrived each year at the same time the Nile flooded. Representing the god Thoth, the ibis became a symbol for creation and the new life the river brought. Thoth was also the god of knowledge and writing. Also, thousands of frogs appeared along the Nile during certain seasons. So Heqet, the frog goddess, stood for fruitfulness and rebirth. The female hippopotamus was Taweret, the popular household goddess of childbirth.

The heron was a common bird found along the Nile in ancient times.

The cobra represented power and kingship, and it could protect a king with its deadly venom. Headdresses of rulers were often adorned with cobras.

Ammut—a god with a crocodile's head, the front of a lion's body, and the rear of a hippo—punished evildoers and devoured the dead. Jackals were scavengers, roaming around to eat leftovers or dead

Endangered Crocs

Ancient Egyptians feared crocodiles, but they also honored the crocodile god, Sobek. According to Herodotus, some Egyptians kept crocodiles as pets. They adorned their crocs with jewelry and mummified them after death.

In modern times hunting and loss of habitat have severely reduced Egypt's Nile crocodile population. The fierce creatures are prized for their skins and meat, as well as for their trophy value. In addition, the Aswan High Dam has largely confined the crocs to regions behind the dam. Once listed as an endangered species, the Nile crocodile is making a comeback due to protection laws.

animals. They were often seen in cemeteries. Thus, the jackal god Anubis presided over ceremonies for the dead.

Besides the cat goddess Bastet, pets were honored members of the household. Dogs were valuable because they helped with hunting. Monkeys and cheetahs were tamed as pets, too. Beloved pets were often made into mummies and buried with their owners. The pets, it was believed, would provide companionship in the afterlife.

ANIMAL LIFE TODAY

Some of the same animals live along the Nile today, though many have become scarce. Crocodiles, for example, used to be plentiful all along the river. Today, they inhabit much of Africa. In the Nile region, however, they mostly live south of the Aswan High Dam. With its powerful, sharp-toothed jaw and its muscular tail, the Nile crocodile can grow to be more than 16 feet (5 m) long. This stealthy predator hides in the water and leaps out to grab large animals that come to drink along the bank.

Hippopotamuses used to roll around on the Nile's muddy riverbanks and slosh in its waters. Today, hippos no longer live in Egypt. They inhabit the Sudd swamplands of Sudan and the lakes and marshes farther south. Bulky and barrel-shaped, hippos may seem awkward on land. However, they can "gallop" as fast as 30 miles (48 km) an hour.

Swamp cats—also called jungle cats or reed cats—live in the Nile Delta and other marshy areas along the Nile. They are yellowish-brown with pointy, black-tufted ears and a short, black-tipped tail. The African wildcat has long

Life as a Hippo

Hippopotamuses are well adapted to their lifestyle. Their skin excretes a red substance that works as a sunscreen. Their eyes, ears, and nostrils are all on top of their head. These openings close when the hippos go underwater. There they swim or walk across the river bottom. For hippos, daytime life and night life are very different. During the day they gather in groups and wallow in the wetlands or the riverside mud. At night they graze for grasses on dry land. This is not a social activity. They graze alone, except for mothers with babies.

African wildcats live in a variety of habitats. Their mottled coat blends in both desert and vegetation.

legs and a long tail with black rings around it. Both these cats look somewhat like domestic cats. They are definitely wild animals, though, and will put up a fierce defense if they feel threatened.

Frogs, turtles, and tortoises are common along the wet banks of the Nile. Several endangered turtle species are found in the Nile Delta. They include loggerhead turtles and green turtles. The Egyptian tortoise is endangered, too. People catch these small, attractive tortoises to sell as pets.

Monitor Lizards

The Nile monitor lizard is a fierce reptile of the Nile region. This large lizard can grow to be 7.5 feet (2.3 m) long. When threatened, it fights with its sharp teeth and claws. It has even been known to use its long tail as a whip.

Birds and Fish of the Nile

Pied kingfishers are often seen perched on branches along the Nile. These black-and-white birds dive into the water and snatch fish with their beaks. Ibises still live along the Nile, and they are fishers, too. Their long, curved bills make good fishing tools. Of the many ibis species along the Nile, the scarlet ibis is the most brilliantly colored.

Flocks of graceful, long-necked flamingos can be seen wading in shallow waters. Flamingos are pink, although they begin life as white birds. The more tiny, pink brine shrimp they eat, the pinker their feathers become!

Every year millions of birds migrate between Europe and Africa along what is called the East African Flyway. They include storks, cranes, and pelicans, as well as eagles, buzzards, and sparrow hawks. On their way

Flamingos feed and wade in the shallow waters of the Nile.

they settle in wetlands along the Nile to feed and rest. Hundreds of thousands of waterbirds spend their winters along the Nile. Among them are large populations of gulls, terns, cormorants, and ducks. For some of these species Egypt is their breeding place.

More than a hundred fish species live in the Nile. Two of the bigger specimens are the Nile tilapia and the Nile perch. Both are tasty. They are the major fish species in Lake Nasser. Tilapia is so popular that it has been introduced into lakes and fish farms all over the world.

Many kinds of catfish live in the Nile, too. They are bottom-feeders, skimming the muddy river bottom for food. The Nile's water is fresh, but some marine, or saltwater, fish live in the delta. They swim in with salty water that washes in from the Mediterranean Sea.

PLANT LIFE

Ancient Egyptians made good use of the papyrus plants that grew along the Nile. The long stems of these water

The Nile Delta is rich with papyrus plants.

Papyrus Weavers

Papyrus marshes are favorite habitats for weaverbirds. These bright yellow birds use papyrus flowers and other plant fibers to weave their intricate, globe-shaped nests. Weaverbirds live and breed in huge colonies. Hundreds of their nests can be seen hanging in or near the swamps.

plants were made into cloth, ropes, and even lightweight boats. Most important, papyrus was used to make a kind of paper. It made a smooth, sturdy writing surface for letters and official documents. Papyrus was so important that it became a symbol for Lower Egypt, the northern kingdom. Upper Egypt's symbol was the lotus, a type of water lily.

Today, a rich variety of plant life flourishes along the Nile. Thickets of papyrus still grow in the Nile Delta, the riverside marshes, and Sudan's swampy Sudd. Tall elephant grass and stiff reeds live in these wetlands, too.

Tropical rain forests grow high in the great lakes region, where the White Nile begins. The same rain-drenched foliage thrives along Ethiopia's Blue Nile as it nears Sudan. Coffee plants and banana, rubber, and bamboo trees are found there.

In riverside regions with less rainfall there are vast expanses of savannah, or dry grasslands. Scattered here and there are bushes and thorny acacia trees. North of Khartoum the Nile enters arid desert where there are few plants, though there are lush date groves along the banks in some places. In both Egypt and Sudan many crops grow alongside the Nile thanks to irrigation.

BOUNTIFUL CROPS

In ancient times Egyptians reaped bountiful harvests from the banks of the Nile. Their major grain crops were barley and a type of wheat called emmer. Other important crops included onions, beans, cucumbers, and lettuce. Dates, figs, melons, pomegranates, and grapes were favorite fruits. Egyptians also grew flax, which they wove into linen for clothing.

Today, farmers along the Nile raise many of the same crops their ancestors did. Agriculture is still a major part of Egypt's economy, and almost all farming takes place along the Nile. There farmers grow wheat, millet, beans, onions, corn, rice, sugarcane, and alfalfa. However, cotton is the main crop. Egypt is the world's largest producer of long-staple, or long-fibered, cotton. As long as the waters continue to flow, the bountiful harvests will continue.

Along the Blue Nile, near ▷▷
Sudan, the landscape
becomes lush and green.

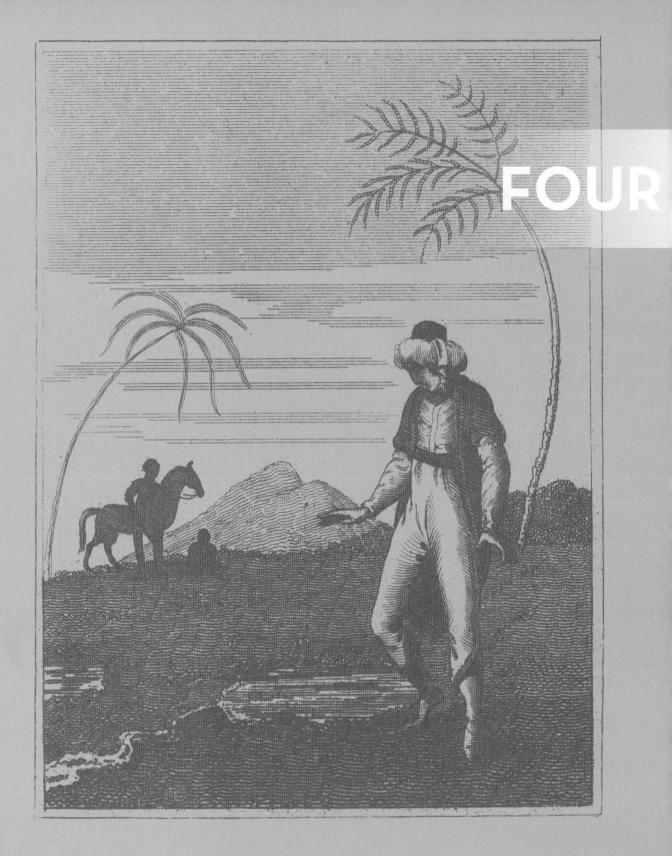

FOUR

Seeking the Great Prize

Where is the source of the Nile? For thousands of years this was one of the greatest unsolved mysteries on earth. Countless explorers tried to find the source but failed. Many people came to accept that it could never be found. The ancient Romans even had a saying: *caput Nili quærere*—Latin for "to seek the head of the Nile." They used the saying to describe a task that was impossible.

Nevertheless, the search went on. By the 1800s the source of the Nile was known among explorers as the Great Prize. Winning that prize would surely earn a person an honored place in history.

◀ *For centuries explorers searched for the source of the Nile River.*

THE MOUNTAINS OF THE MOON

In the fifth century B.C.E. the Greek historian Herodotus traveled up the Nile. He got as far as Elephantine Island, near Aswan. On the way he met a priest who told him where the Nile began. It sprang, he said, from bottomless fountains deep inside two mountains.

But where were those mountains? The search continued. The ancient Greek conqueror Alexander the Great and the Roman emperor Julius Caesar both tried to find them. In the first century C.E. the Roman emperor Nero sent an expedition south to follow the Nile to its source. The men became hopelessly tangled up in the immense Sudd swamp and returned, having failed in their mission.

Not long after that a Greek merchant named Diogenes was sailing from India back to Greece. His ship blew off course, and he landed on the coast of Africa. Diogenes trekked inland and discovered a mountain range whose peaks seemed to be shrouded in snow. Because the mountains were white, Diogenes said, local people called them the Mountains of the Moon.

The Greek geographer Ptolemy accepted Diogenes' report and drew his own conclusions. Around 150 C.E. Ptolemy wrote that the melting snow from the mountains was the source of the Nile. Ptolemy began including the Mountains of the Moon on his maps. He showed rivers running from the mountains into lakes from which the Nile flowed. For centuries this scheme was accepted as true.

Master Mapmaker

Ptolemy (ca. 100–ca. 170) was one of the greatest geographers of the ancient world. His workplace was Alexandria, Egypt, a center of Greek culture and learning. Among his greatest works was his *Geographike hyphegesis*. In this set of books, dated at about 150 C.E., Ptolemy brought together all the geographic knowledge of his time. Maps in the *Geographike hyphegesis* showed all the regions of the world he knew. That included the Mountains of the Moon, where he believed the source of the Nile lay. In 1406 Ptolemy's *Geographike hyphegesis* was translated from Greek into Latin. Then it became available to scholars throughout Europe.

TRACKING THE BLUE NILE

Until the 1600s no one was aware that the Nile had two sources. Then two travelers raised the suspicion that the Nile rose in Abyssinia—modern-day Ethiopia. The first of those travelers was Pedro Páez, a Portuguese priest of the Jesuit religious order. He ventured into Ethiopia hoping to convert people from the Ethiopian Orthodox Church to Roman Catholicism.

In 1618 Páez came upon not only Lake Tana but also the spring whose waters flow into it. Páez declared that he had seen the source of the Blue Nile and of the great Nile River itself. Thrilled at his discovery, he wrote, "I cannot express my delight in seeing that which . . . Alexander and Julius Caesar so strongly and so unavailingly desired to know."

James Bruce wrote of his explorations and discoveries in Travels to Discover the Source of the Nile.

Páez was indeed the first European to reach the source of the Blue Nile. Perhaps because he was a priest and not an explorer, though, his discovery went unnoticed. More than a century later a daring Scottish explorer named James Bruce set out to find the source of the Nile. He was aware that Páez claimed to have found the source. However, he challenged Páez's claim, saying it was made up.

In 1770, after many adventures and near-death ordeals, Bruce reached Lake Tana. He was the first explorer to map the lake and follow the Blue Nile to Khartoum and on to the Nile Delta.

Back in England Bruce reported his findings, but people laughed at him. They did not believe the wild tales he told of his travels. Furthermore, they did not believe the Nile's source lay in Abyssinia. They still insisted that the true source was in the upper reaches of the White Nile.

Actually, in Khartoum Bruce had seen another river flowing into the Nile. Realizing he may have tracked the wrong river, his heart sank. Nevertheless, he insisted that Lake Tana was the source the ancient explorers were seeking. Bruce retired to Scotland, broken and disappointed. Long after his death he received credit for his discovery. Meanwhile, explorers continued to focus on the White Nile.

THE WHITE NILE: TRIUMPH AND TRAGEDY

Over the years the mystery of the Nile's source grew ever more intriguing. In the mid-1800s that mystery would at last be solved.

In June 1857 two British officers—Richard Burton and John Hanning Speke—set off on an expedition to find the source of the Nile. All efforts to find the source by boating up the river had failed. So Burton and Speke decided to travel overland from the East African coast. Eight months later they became the first Europeans to reach Lake Tanganyika. Burton was sure this was the source of the Nile.

Richard Burton

Richard Francis Burton (1821–1890) was a swashbuckling adventurer who explored many regions of Africa and the Middle East. He was the first European to visit the Muslim holy city of Mecca in what is now Saudi Arabia. Of all Burton's expeditions, the most famous is his search for the Nile. Proficient in many languages, Burton was the first to translate *The Thousand and One Nights* from Arabic into English. This collection of 1,001 stories is often called *The Arabian Nights*.

By this time both men were racked with disease. Burton, suffering from malaria, could hardly walk. Speke was almost blind due to an infection. The two were not getting along, either. Their personality differences had spilled over into professional jealousy, and they split up.

Speke headed north on his own and, in July 1858, reached a huge body of water. He named it Lake Victoria, after the British queen. Speke identified the lake as the source of the Nile, and he was right. However, he himself did not explore the lake or even see the Nile pouring out of it.

Burton shrugged off Speke's discovery, insisting on Lake Tanganyika as the true source. Unbeknownst to Burton, Speke had been burning with resentment for years. Speke unleashed a torrent of insults at Burton, and the friendship of the longtime comrades lapsed into a bitterness beyond repair.

John Hanning Speke

John Hanning Speke (1827–1864) was a British army officer who served in India. During his time off he explored the Himalaya Mountains and even ventured into Tibet. In 1855 Speke joined Richard Burton's expedition to Somalia. Both men were severely wounded there. In 1856 the two teamed up to seek the source of the Nile in east-central Africa. There Speke became the first European to reach Lake Victoria, the White Nile's source. England's Royal Geographical Society arranged for Speke and Burton to debate about the source. However, Speke died just before the debate. No one is certain whether his death was an accident or suicide.

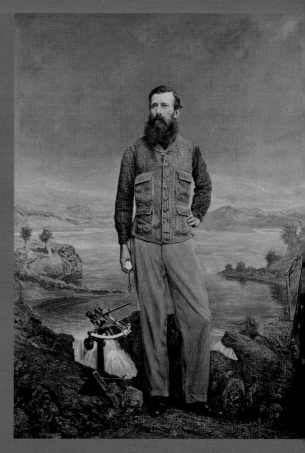

THE DUEL FOR THE NILE

Back in England Speke announced his discovery and was hailed as a hero. Burton, stung by Speke's treachery, published a book belittling his former partner. Proclaiming himself the superstar of the expedition, Burton still insisted on Lake Tanganyika as the Nile's source. To make matters worse, Speke was awarded funds to return to Lake Victoria and confirm that it was the White Nile's source.

The explorers' rivalry created great publicity and fueled a lot of gossip. In September 1864 Burton and Speke were scheduled to hold a public debate on the issue in Bath, England. Burton would argue for Lake Tanganyika, and Speke would champion Lake Victoria. The dispute became known as the Nile Duel. Scientists, explorers, and ordinary people alike were anxious to follow the great debate.

Mysteriously, just one day before the debate, Speke was allegedly shot and killed by his own gun in a hunting accident. In spite of their disagreements, Burton was grieved. Knowing Speke was an expert with firearms, he imagined that his rival may have committed suicide.

STANLEY AND LIVINGSTONE

It would seem that the search for the source of the Nile had come to an end. Nevertheless, two other notable explorers kept on looking. One was the Scottish explorer and missionary David Livingstone.

In Livingstone's mind both Burton and Speke were foolishly mistaken about the Nile's source. Livingstone set out on his own quest in 1866. All he found, though, was the Lualaba River, in present-day Congo. Livingstone convinced himself that this was the headstream of the Nile. By this time his body was as unbalanced as his mind. Exhausted and racked with disease, he could barely stand up.

Months and years passed, and no one ever heard from Livingstone. Most people figured he was dead. However, a shrewd newspaper editor saw this as a chance to publish some good stories. As a publicity stunt the *New York Herald* sent the journalist Henry Morton Stanley to find Livingstone. Stanley was to send back progress reports that newspaper readers could enjoy.

Lost and Found

This is how Henry Stanley described his meeting with David Livingstone:

As I advanced slowly towards him I noticed he was pale, that he looked wearied and wan, that he had grey whiskers and moustache, that he wore a bluish cloth cap with a faded gold band on a red ground round it, and that he had on a red-sleeved waistcoat, and a pair of grey tweed trousers.

I would have run to him, only I was a coward in the presence of such a mob—would have embraced him, but that I did not know how he would receive me; so I did what moral cowardice and false pride suggested was the best thing—walked deliberately to him, took off my hat, and said: "Dr. Livingstone, I presume?"

—from *How I Found Livingstone,* by Henry Morton Stanley, 1871

Setting out in 1869, Stanley combed the jungles of central Africa. At last, in 1871, he came upon the old man and uttered his now-famous comment: "Dr. Livingstone, I presume?" Stanley presumed correctly. Livingstone regained his strength, and the two took off together on that seemingly endless quest—to find the source of the Nile. In 1873 Livingstone died of malaria and dysentery in Africa.

THOSE WHITE MOUNTAINS

Stanley went on to explore more of Africa. In 1889 he was trekking near Lake Victoria when he came upon a towering mountain range. The mountains rose so high that clouds hid their summits. Suddenly, the clouds cleared, and Stanley could see glistening white peaks. These, he declared, were the fabled Mountains of the Moon.

This mountain range, rising on the border of Uganda and the Congo, is now known as the Ruwenzori Mountains. And they are ice capped, not snowcapped. Glaciers, rather than snow, account for their dazzling whiteness.

Are these really the white mountains that Diogenes found in ancient times? No one really knows, although it is popularly assumed that they are. With Stanley's discovery, the search for the source of the Nile had come full circle—back to the Mountains of the Moon.

AN ETERNAL QUEST?

For modern-day adventurers the Nile River remains a mystery and a challenge. Establishing the sources of the Nile did not put the quests

The ice capped peaks of the Ruwenzori Mountains.

to rest. The next challenge became a test of courage. One after another, expeditions set out in boats to navigate the river from source to sea.

In 2004 the geologist Pasquale Scaturro and the filmmaker Gordon Banks were the first to travel the Blue Nile from Lake Tana to the Mediterranean Sea. That same year the South Africans Hendri Coetzee and Peter Meredith led a team down the White Nile. They were the first to navigate the river from Lake Victoria to the Mediterranean.

Perhaps the most newsworthy Nile expedition in modern times took place in 2006. Neil McGrigor led a team of explorers from Great Britain and New Zealand up the Nile and far beyond Lake Victoria. Their goal was a shocking one—to find the "true source" of the Nile. They were certain that the White Nile's headwaters were even more distant than anyone had thought before. Deep in the forests of Rwanda they found the trickle of water they were seeking.

Neil McGrigor (center) celebrates with members of his exploration team at the newly found source of the Nile.

"We Know We Are Correct"

Cam McLeay, coleader of the 2006 expedition to the source of the Nile, made these comments about the team's measurements:

We know we are correct because we have studied the maps in detail and have now physically traced the longest source on the ground. We've measured the river electronically using GPS tracks and now have the electronic data to prove the Nile is 6,719 kilometers [4,175 miles] in length.

This discovery added many more miles to the Nile's total length. Geographers worldwide have not fully accepted the team's findings. However, the explorers took measurements using sophisticated global positioning system (GPS) equipment. Thus, they were able to establish distances more accurately than anyone had ever done before. In any case, future explorers will surely continue to seek out the mysteries of the Nile.

FIVE

Living with the Flow

Most ancient peoples devised calendars based on the cycles of the sun or moon. Ancient Egyptians, however, marked time in a different way. Their calendar was based on the annual cycles of the Nile River.

SEASONS OF THE NILE

Year in and year out, daily life in ancient Egypt was tied to the Nile. The rise and fall of the great river broke the year into three distinct seasons.

The new year began in mid-June with the season of Akhet, meaning "inundation." That was the season of the annual flooding, or inundation, of the Nile. At this time of year seasonal rainwater from the Ethiopian highlands came gushing down the Blue Nile. The floodwaters covered Egypt's riverside lowlands, called the **floodplain**, leaving mineral-rich sediment across the land. The rich, black topsoil would guarantee abundant crops.

◄ *The people who live along the Nile rely on the river for their agricultural needs, as well as for the transportation of goods.*

Hapy, God of the Nile

Ancient Egyptians honored Hapy as the god of the Nile. It was Hapy who made the river swell and flood every year, ensuring bountiful crops. Hapy's name means "running one." That probably refers to the running current of the Nile.

Egyptians saw this time as the beginning of new life—a kind of new creation. They welcomed their new year with five days of rituals and celebrations. These festivities also honored the birthdays of their most important gods.

Since the countryside was flooded during Akhet, people traveled around in boats. Fishing was an important activity then. The plentiful fish catches from the swollen Nile made up a major part of the common people's diet.

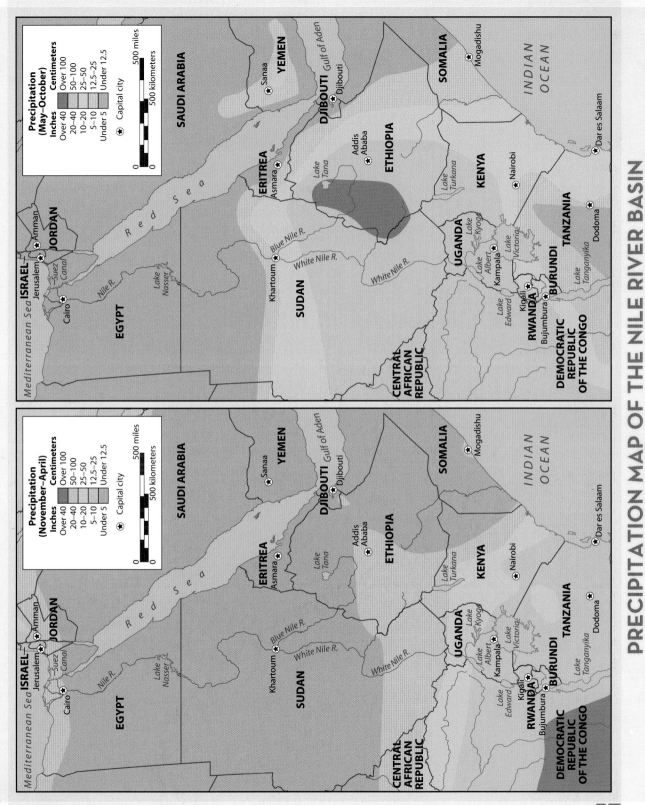

PRECIPITATION MAP OF THE NILE RIVER BASIN

SOWING AND HARVESTING

Gradually the floodwaters receded, leaving the fields moist, fertile, and ready for planting. In mid-October the season of Proyet, meaning "emergence," began. That was when the land emerged from the waters. Proyet was the season for sowing seeds, and farmers could easily plow and dig the soft soil. After depositing the seeds by hand, they had goats walk over the sowed area. This pushed the seeds down into the soil so hungry birds could not get to them.

Once the crops began to grow, they needed to be watered. For that people dug canals, or long ditches, from the Nile out to their fields. To lift the water from the canals, they used the shadoof. This was a long pole mounted on a crossbeam, like a seesaw. On one end of the pole was a bucket, and on the other end was a heavy weight. Farmers filled the bucket by dipping it into the canal. Then they swung the pole around and emptied the water onto their crops. Even today, some farmers in Egypt use the shadoof to water their fields.

Shomu, the dry season, began in mid-February. This was the time for the harvest. Workers went through the fields with curved-blade sickles, cutting the tall stalks of ripened grain. Then they threshed and winnowed the grain to separate the edible morsels from the hulls. After the harvest farmers spent time repairing their canals before the floodwaters arrived again.

Thanks to the life-giving waters of the Nile, the ancient Egyptians developed a rich, stable culture. The Nile played a major role in their

Egyptian farmers ▷▷
use a shadoof to lift
water from the Nile.

Measuring the Floods

During the flood season, the Nile's water level rose an average of 27 feet (8.2 m). Egyptians forecasted their crop yields by measuring the Nile's flood level with a device called a nilometer. The simplest nilometer was a stone column rising out of the water, with notches marking various heights. An example still exists on Cairo's Roda Island. Another type of nilometer was a series of steps leading down to the water, with height markings alongside them. One can be seen on Aswan's Elephantine Island (above).

way of life, as well as in their religion and their economy. With such abundant crops, Egypt was able to export wheat, flax, and other products to other lands. This brought wealth to the kingdom, enabling the pharaohs to build magnificent monuments that still stand today. From this Nile-fed land rose one of the greatest ancient civilizations in the world.

NUBIANS AND THE NILE

South of ancient Egypt, another great culture flourished along the Nile. It was the ancient kingdom of Nubia. Covering southern Egypt and northern Sudan, Nubia extended roughly from present-day Aswan to Khartoum. The Nubian civilization was Africa's earliest known black culture, with a history reaching back more than five thousand years.

For the Nubians the Nile did not play as great a role as it did for the Egyptians. That was because Nubia did not rely as heavily on agriculture. Rich in natural resources and trade networks, Nubia was a land of great wealth. Its products and trade goods were prized in faraway markets.

The common people of Nubia lived by hunting, gathering wild plants, and farming. Nubian farmers moved water using a *sakieh*, or waterwheel. This wheel stood parallel to the ground, rather than upright. Cattle harnessed to the wheel walked around in a circle to turn it. On the outer edge were buckets that picked up water and emptied it into a trough or pipe. With this device farmers could

irrigate land farther from the Nile and also move water up to higher ground. This enabled them to have three crop cycles a year, in contrast to Egypt's one annual growing season.

Millet, wheat, and barley were the Nubians' major food crops. Farmers also raised beans, tobacco, lentils, peas, and watermelons. They sold or traded these crops with Egyptians and other people. Using irrigation water from the Nile during dry seasons, Nubians could also grow dates, mangoes, and citrus trees.

Egyptians regularly traveled up the Nile to trade with Nubia. Gold, copper, and stone from Nubian mines were useful in making ornaments and building monuments. Nubians were also expert traders who acquired exotic items from central Africa. Ivory, ebony wood, incense, precious oils, leopard skins, monkeys, giraffes, and ostrich feathers—all were available from Nubian merchants. Egyptian traders were thrilled to procure these rare and wonderful goods. After loading up their boats in Nubia, they sailed back down the Nile, into Egypt.

◄◄ *Nubian farmers used waterwheels to irrigate their fields.*

IMPROVING ON NATURE

As the centuries passed, people along the Nile saw many rulers come and go. Greek and Roman empires and Christian and Muslim cultures spread their influence across the land. All the while, though, the annual rise and fall of the Nile marked the steady rhythm of everyday life. That rhythm began to change in the 1800s.

As modern engineering advanced, people's skill in building dams improved as well. In the 1800s Egypt began planning dam projects to improve irrigation and control flooding. The natural, seasonal flow of the Nile had nourished Egypt for thousands of years. Yet nature had its drawbacks. If Ethiopia's annual rains were especially heavy, devastating floods wiped out entire villages along the Nile. If the rains were light, the Nile could not provide enough water and silt to nourish the crops.

Egypt's first dam project, called the Delta Barrage, was completed in 1861. It involved building a type of dam across the head of the Nile Delta. The **barrage** raised the water level farther upstream to create more irrigation water for farms. This was the first modern irrigation project on the Nile. The Assyut Barrage, farther upstream, opened in 1902, and others followed in the years to come.

The first dam built at Aswan was completed in 1902. It included a series of locks through which boats could travel between higher and lower water levels. The dam was enlarged twice, in 1911 and 1934. Meanwhile, in Sudan a dam was completed on the Blue Nile near Sennar in 1925. This made it possible to irrigate the Gezira plain, south of Khartoum. That plain is now Sudan's richest farming region, specializing in cotton.

THE ASWAN HIGH DAM

The Aswan High Dam was the most gigantic dam project ever. It was built for three major reasons: to prevent floods; to create a regular, year-round supply of irrigation water; and to generate hydroelectric power. Behind the dam the backed-up waters created massive Lake Nasser. It extends across the Egypt-Sudan border.

The Aswan High Dam was built to regulate yearly floods as well as to create a reservoir with the capacity to provide water during a drought.

Moving Mountains

A team of engineers and laborers from many countries saved the temples at Abu Simbel. Working from the top of the mountain downward, they cut the monuments into huge blocks of stone. In all the two temples were cut into about 16,000 blocks. One by one, workers moved them to higher ground more than 200 feet (61 m) away. There the temples were reassembled in their original form. More than fifty countries donated funds for the project, which cost about $80 million.

Construction of the dam (1959–1970) posed huge problems. Lake Nasser would flood thousands of square miles of land in Egypt and Sudan. To clear that land, more than 90,000 Egyptian and Sudanese-Nubian people were uprooted and resettled in other areas of Egypt and Sudan amid demonstrations and conflict.

Another relocation project was undertaken, too. Lake Nasser would flood hundreds of ancient temples and tombs. Among those, the largest were two temples at Abu Simbel. Pharaoh Ramses II had built them on a mountainside in the 1200s B.C.E. Guarding the entrance to the Great Temple were four seated statues of Ramses, each about 66 feet (20 m) high. Beyond the entrance were three cavernous halls full of statues and wall paintings. At the entrance to the smaller temple nearby stood four statues of Ramses and two figures of his wife, Nefertari.

Saving the temples would be a tremendous task. To do this, Egypt teamed up with the United Nations Educational, Scientific, and Cultural Organization (UNESCO). Under UNESCO's guidance, hundreds of archaeologists and engineers came in to move the monuments. They cut huge blocks of stone out of the mountainside and put them back together on higher ground.

Moving the Abu Simbel temples was just part of the rescue operation. In all, twenty monuments in Egypt and four in Sudan were moved or granted to countries that helped with the project. Many other archaeological sites were left to be submerged under the waters of Lake Nasser. There simply was not enough time or money to save them all.

Who Gets the Water?

Water from ten countries ends up in the Nile. All those countries have water needs. However, Egypt and Sudan, as the main users of Nile water, have governed its use for more than seventy years. In 1929 the two nations drew up the Nile Waters Agreement and revised it as the Nile Waters Treaty in 1959.

The treaty was based on an average Nile flow of 84 billion cubic meters (2,966 billion cubic feet) a year as measured at Aswan. Out of that, Egypt was allocated 55.5 bcm (1,960 bcf) a year and Sudan 18.5 bcm (653 bcf). It was estimated that the remaining 10 bcm (353 bcf) evaporated or seeped into the ground. Other countries would have to get Egypt's and Sudan's approval for projects that would affect the Nile's flow. Understandably, other countries in the Nile Basin were not happy with this agreement. They considered it illegal. Ethiopia announced that it would develop water projects on the Blue Nile as it saw fit, based on the notion of sovereign rights.

Finally, in 1999 the ten countries in the Nile's watershed agreed to form the Nile Basin Initiative (NBI) for cooperation on the development and use of the river. A number of ongoing projects in various countries added to the pressure to achieve a new, comprehensive agreement. In 2007 NBI member nations were nearing a new pact to replace the 1959 treaty, though there remained some key sticking points.

Irrigation channels allow the Nile's waters to flow freely through the fields and allow farmers to have multiple plantings per year.

DIFFERENT WAYS OF LIFE

In the space of a decade, thousands of years of life along the Nile was changed forever. Lake Nasser stored water and regulated its flow, putting an end to the annual flooding of the Nile in Egypt. Since ancient times Egyptian farmers had shaped their lives around the Nile's yearly cycle. Now their farming methods changed dramatically. Instead of one annual planting, they could sow crops several times a year. With a steady flow of Nile water, they could irrigate those crops year round.

A Bedouin woman tends her sheep in a semi-arid region of Egypt.

The Aswan High Dam vastly improved farming methods. Yet people still searched for ways to get the maximum benefit from the Nile's waters. One glaring problem was southern Sudan's vast, swampy Sudd region. About half of the White Nile's waters evaporated during their sluggish, year-long passage through the swamp. Surely there was a way to offset that tremendous loss of water.

In 1978 Sudan and Egypt launched a joint canal project. They would build the 225-mile (360-km) Jonglei Canal. It would bypass the Sudd, carrying water from south of the swamp to north of it. The water would then move at a higher speed and in a narrow channel, thus avoiding undue evaporative losses. Not only would precious water be saved, but irrigation along the canal would create more fertile cropland. Unfortunately, a civil war broke out in Sudan in 1983, in part due to disputes over this project. With the canal almost three-fourths built, construction ground to a halt.

If completed, the Jonglei Canal would change the lifestyles of local peoples, many of whom are nomadic herders. The canal cuts through a region with an annual cycle of heavy rains and flooding. During the eight-month rainy season people and their cattle leave the area and move to higher ground. The canal, at 245 feet (75 m) wide, would capture the floodwaters so people could stay and farm year round. The Sudd would shrink, too, freeing up more land for farming. But the canal would also change the ecological balance of the region and, possibly, the rainfall patterns in and around the Sudd.

Political unrest in Sudan continues into the twenty-first century. From time to time Egyptian and Sudanese officials speak of resuming the canal project. However, it remains controversial and is unlikely to be completed.

SIX

Preserving the Waters

Few people doubt the benefits of the dams on the Nile River. Since the Aswan High Dam opened in 1970, Egypt's farm income has doubled. Heavy rains in 1973 could have caused devastating floods. However, with the Aswan Dam holding the floodwaters back in Lake Nasser, flooding was prevented.

The dam protects farmers from the effects of drought, too. In the 1970s and 1980s droughts in Ethiopia threatened to cause severe water shortages. By 1988 the water level in Lake Nasser had become dangerously low. A heavy rainfall later that year helped replenish the lake. But without the dam gradually releasing water during the years of drought, crops would have shriveled, leaving millions of Egyptians without food.

The Aswan Dam also generates hydroelectric power for Egyptians who would otherwise be without electricity. Easier boat travel on the Nile is another benefit. However, dams at Aswan and elsewhere along the Nile have also had enormous impacts on the environment.

◂ *The conservation of the Nile River basin has a direct effect on the peoples and wildlife of the region.*

No More Silt

For thousands of years nutrient-rich silt flowing down the Nile fertilized Egypt's croplands. Now that silt is trapped in Lake Nasser. This has several negative consequences. Without the silt deposits, Egyptian farmland lacks the rich topsoil that made it so fertile. Now farmers must use chemical fertilizers. This is not just an added expense for impoverished farmers. The fertilizers also pollute the river and groundwater with chemicals.

The lack of silt results in soil erosion, too. Deposits of silt used to build up the banks of the Nile. Now the riverbanks are eroding, washed away by the Nile's flow. The Nile Delta is also suffering from erosion. Soil along both the coastline and the delta streams have been wearing away since the Aswan Dam opened. At the same time, stretches of the Nile upstream from Lake Nasser are often clogged with silt.

The absence of silt has also affected fish populations. Nutrients in the silt are a major food source for phytoplankton—tiny floating water plants. Phytoplankton, in turn, is an important food for sardines and other fish in the Mediterranean Sea. Dense masses of phytoplankton once thrived in the waters at the mouth of the Nile. The plants nourished a huge population of sardines. For fishing communities in the Mediterranean those sardines were a valuable source of income. Less silt meant less phytoplankton, and sardine fisheries dropped off drastically as a result.

Shores of the Nile erode over time due to the lack of silt to build up the riverbanks.

SALTWATER IN THE DELTA

Nile waters used to surge downstream with tremendous force, gushing out into the salty Mediterranean Sea. Now, thanks to the Aswan High Dam, the force of the Nile's flow is more gentle and steady. As a result saltwater from the Mediterranean is able to force its way up the Nile.

With saltier soil, farmland in the once-fertile Nile Delta has become much less productive. Delta lakes and streams have a much higher salt content, too. This creates saltier irrigation water and reduces fish life.

Water hyacinth is a fast-growing waterweed that chokes the living environment of the Nile River.

WATERWEED CONTROL

Another environmental problem in the Nile River system is water-weeds—especially the water hyacinth. It is considered the world's worst waterweed. It grows and spreads quickly, forming dense mats of floating foliage.

The water hyacinth is native to South America. No one is sure exactly how it got to Africa. Some people consider it a decorative plant, so someone probably brought it in to add to an ornamental water garden. As an "invader," rather than a native plant, water hyacinth is known as an invasive species.

A Pesky Plant Pest

Water hyacinth is an aggressive plant. It crowds out other water plants and prevents oxygen from reaching below the water's surface. In Lake Victoria water hyacinth has eliminated dozens of fish species by blocking their oxygen supply. The pesky weed also interferes with boating and clogs hydroelectric plants. It slows the flow of water, too. This creates an ideal breeding ground for mosquitoes, which carry malaria and other diseases.

West Nile Virus

West Nile virus is a virus that mainly infects birds. Other animals, including humans, may also be infected. Humans usually contract the virus by being bitten by an infected mosquito. Symptoms of the illness it causes in humans, West Nile encephalitis, are similar to common flu symptoms, and no cure has yet been developed. How did West Nile virus get its name? The disease was first diagnosed in a human in the West Nile District of Uganda, located on the west bank of the White Nile River. This took place in 1937. West Nile virus first appeared in North America in 1999.

Water hyacinth is a problem not only in Egypt and Sudan but also in Uganda and other countries in the Nile Basin. Lake Victoria, the source of the White Nile, has suffered serious infestations of the weed. By the 1990s hundreds of fishing villages around the lake were abandoned. It was so clogged with water hyacinth that people simply could not move their fishing boats out into the lake. Ships could not dock at lakeside ports, either.

Several countries are trying to eliminate water hyacinth with mechanical equipment and chemical weed killers. However, nothing has worked as well as biological control. That involves releasing beetles called water hyacinth weevils into infested waterways. These little insects have a voracious appetite for water hyacinths. By the year 2000 the weevils had dramatically reduced the weeds in Lake Victoria. Sudan, too, has controlled its water hyacinth problem by using weevils.

Invasive Fish

Weeds are not the only invasive species in the Nile system. Invasive fish species live there, too. Nile perch were introduced into Lake Victoria in the 1950s to boost commercial fishing. Since then the perch have become the dominant fish in the lake. Now they are considered a **biodiversity** disaster. The perch are said to have eliminated

more than three hundred of the lake's native species. First, they ate up their favorite large fish species. Then, they turned to shrimp, minnows, and smaller fish. The perch have boosted the exports of large fishing companies. However, they do not benefit the residents of small, lakeside fishing villages.

WETLAND PROTECTION

The Sudd swamp in Sudan is often seen as an obstacle to the White Nile's flow. However, environmentalists see it as a valuable wetland. The Sudd supports woodlands and grasslands, as well as aquatic plants and animals. It is a habitat for crocodiles, hippopotamuses, and waterbirds. Gazelles, elephants, and other wildlife go there to drink. Many animal herds also migrate to the Sudd during dry

A yellow-billed stork and a small Nile crocodile share the shallows of the Nile River.

seasons. In addition, the wetland provides a vital water supply for people and their cattle. The Sudd may also contribute to important rainfall patterns in the region.

One potential threat to the Sudd would be the completion of the Jonglei Canal around the swamp. Environmentalists oppose the canal because it would disrupt the region's natural ecosystems and create a huge barrier to movement across the region. Many local people oppose the canal, too, including the Dinka and Nuer tribespeople. These nomadic herders depend on the Sudd's floodwaters to renew grasslands where their cattle graze. The canal might force them to give up their traditional lifestyle and settle down as farmers. That might help Sudan's economy, but it would destroy a way of life.

Another threat to the Sudd is oil drilling. The swamp sits atop valuable oil deposits, and drilling has already caused the pollution of its waters. In 2006 Sudan declared the Sudd a Wetland of International Importance. Environmentalists hope this move will lead to more protection for the Sudd. Nevertheless, Sudan has not yet developed an environmental protection policy, and oil brings in much-needed income. As of 2007 several foreign companies were exploring or drilling for oil in the Sudd.

OUTLOOK FOR THE FUTURE

Many other environmental problems plague the Nile. With few regulations in place, factories release chemical wastes into the river. Sewage from cities and villages enters the Nile, too, causing cholera, typhoid, and other diseases. Deforestation is another problem. As trees are cut for firewood and farming, soil is no longer held in place. The eroding soil then washes into the waterways. These are just a few of the threats to the Nile's future.

The ten countries in the Nile Basin are among the poorest in the world. Water scarcity is a big part of their poverty problem. The World Health Organization (WHO) reports that more than half of

Shares of the Nile Basin

Country	% of Country in the Basin	% of the Total Basin
Burundi	47.6	0.4
DRC*	0.9	0.7
Egypt	32.6	10.5
Eritrea	20.5	0.8
Ethiopia	32.4	11.7
Kenya	7.9	1.5
Rwanda	75.5	0.7
Sudan	79.0	63.6
Tanzania	8.9	2.7
Uganda	98.0	7.4

*DRC = Democratic Republic of the Congo

Africa's population lacks safe drinking water. Populations in the Nile Basin countries could double by the mid-twenty-first century. Their people will need a tremendous amount of water for drinking, irrigation, fisheries, and hydroelectric power. Such needs could strain the Nile River system to its limits.

International officials warn that "water wars" are likely to be Africa's next conflicts. In the past Egypt has even threatened military action against countries planning large water projects on the Nile. Clearly, the water needs of individual countries must be balanced against the welfare of their neighbors. Only through international cooperation can this be done.

The Nile Basin Initiative (NBI), the United Nations Environment Programme (UNEP), and several other international organizations are working on cooperative plans for developing and sharing Nile waters. These plans include safeguards for the environment. If they succeed, the longest river on earth may continue to bestow its life-giving waters on generations to come.

The Nile flows through poverty-ridden countries, where few restrictions are in place to conserve the precious waters.

Glossary

barrage a low, submersible dam used to block or divert water from reaching an ocean

biodiversity the variety and number of plant and animal species living in an environment

drainage basin a large area of land whose rainwater or melting snow runs downhill into a body of water; also called a watershed

ecosystems communities of organisms functioning together within their environments

floodplain level land alongside a river whose soil is built up from sediments deposited by the river; also holds water overflow during flooding

headwaters the original point from which a lake's or river's waters flow; the most distant source of its waters

monsoon heavy rainfall and high winds that occur annually in parts of Africa and Asia

silt tiny, mineral-rich particles of soil carried by a river

tributaries rivers or streams that flow into a larger river

watershed high ground that divides one drainage basin from another; the term can also refer to the drainage basin itself

Fast Facts

Name: Nile River (Arabic: Bahr an-Nil)

Major tributaries: Blue Nile, White Nile

Sources: Lake Tana, Ethiopia (Blue Nile); Lake Victoria, east-central Africa (White Nile)

Mouth: Mediterranean Sea

Mediterranean Sea

Countries crossed: Egypt, Sudan

Basin countries: Burundi, the Democratic Republic of the Congo, Egypt, Eritrea, Ethiopia, Kenya, Rwanda, Sudan, Tanzania, Uganda

Basin population: (est.)160 million (1990 est.; 300 million, 2010 est.)

Drainage area: (est.)1,293,000 square miles (3,349,000 sq km)

Dates of source discoveries: 1770 (Blue Nile), 1858 (White Nile)

Source discoverers: James Bruce (Blue Nile), John Hanning Speke (White Nile)

Length: 4,160 miles (6,695 km) per U.S. Geological Survey
  4,175 miles (6,719 km) per 2006 expedition
  4,187 miles (6,738 km) per Egypt State Information Service

Major cities: Cairo, Giza, Tanta, Luxor (ancient Thebes), Asyut, and Aswan, Egypt; Atbara, Omdurman, Karima, Khartoum, and Khartoum North, Sudan; Lake Tana: Bahir Dar, Ethiopia; Lake Victoria: Kisumu, Kenya; Kampala and Entebbe, Uganda; Mwanza, Tanzania

Major dams: Aswan High Dam, on the Nile River near Aswan, Egypt; Sennar Dam at Sennar and Roseires Dam near Roseires, on the Blue Nile; Owen Falls Dam, on the White Nile near Lake Victoria, Uganda; Jebel Aulia Dam on the White Nile at Jebel Aulia, Sudan

Lake Tana

Elephantine Island

Major islands: Roda (Rawdah) and Zamalek in Cairo; Elephantine Island at Aswan; Tuti Island at Khartoum

Animals: Crocodiles, monitor lizards, hippopotamuses, Nile perch, tilapia, a variety of water-birds

Plants: Papyrus, reeds, grasses, water hyacinth (invasive)

Famous monuments: Pyramids and the Great Sphinx in Giza; temples of Abu Simbel; temples of Luxor and Karnak; tombs and monuments of Thebes; Meroë pyramids (Sudan)

Economic benefits: Irrigation water, domestic water, soil nutrients, hydroelectric power, transportation, fisheries

Political issues: International competition for water use, disputes over water-management schemes

Environmental threats: Soil erosion, wetland loss, invasive plant and animal species, industrial and sewage pollution, new dam construction

Cultural threats: Water damage to ancient monuments, loss of traditional lifestyles

Meroë Pyramids

Find Out More

....
BOOKS
....

Banting, Erinn. *The Nile River: The Longest River in the World*. New York: Weigl Publishers, 2004.

Bowden, Rob. *Settlements of the River Nile*. Chicago: Heinemann Library Press, 2005.

Graf, Mike. *The Nile River*. Mankato, MN: Capstone Press, 2006.

Millard, Anne, and Steve Noon (illustrator). *The Story of the Nile: A Journey Through Time on the World's Longest River*. New York: DK Children, 2003.

Nardo, Don. *People of the Nile: Rhythms of Daily Life*. San Diego: Lucent Books, 2005.

Parks, Peggy J. *Aswan High Dam*. San Diego: Blackbirch Press, 2004.

....
WEB SITES
....

The Animals of Ancient Egypt

www.thekeep.org/~Ekunoichi/kunoichi/themestream/
egypt_animals.html

Visit this Web site to learn about animals and their special roles in the ancient Egyptian religion.

Nubia in Modern and Ancient Times

touregypt.net/historicalessays/nubia.htm

Visit this Web site for information on Nubian culture, traditions, history, and monuments.

The River Nile Homepage

www.utdallas.edu/geosciences/remsens/Nile/index.html

For information on the Nile's sections, sources, tributaries, and importance visit the River Nile homepage.

Index

Page numbers in **boldface** are illustrations and charts.

ABOUT THE AUTHOR

Ann Heinrichs loves traveling to faraway places. Alongside the Nile River in Egypt she watched farmers working amid the lush growth of the riverbank. In Ethiopia she boated across Lake Tana, watched the Blue Nile spill out of the lake, and explored the base of the Blue Nile Falls. Writing this book brought back many memories of beautiful landscapes and warm, friendly people. Heinrichs grew up roaming the woods behind her home in Fort Smith, Arkansas. Now she lives in Chicago, Illinois. She is the author of more than two hundred books for children and young adults.